Sound Trackers

Jazz

SOUND TRACKERS – JAZZ
was produced by

David West ⚇ Children's Books
7 Princeton Court
55 Felsham Road
London SW15 1AZ

Designer: Rob Shone
Picture Research: Fiona Thorne
Editor: James Pickering

First published in Great Britain in 2002 by
Heinemann Library, Halley Court, Jordan Hill, Oxford OX2 8EJ, a division of
Reed Educational and Professional Publishing Limited.

OXFORD MELBOURNE AUCKLAND
JOHANNESBURG BLANTYRE GABORONE
IBADAN PORTSMOUTH (NH) USA CHICAGO

06 05 04 03 02
10 9 8 7 6 5 4 3 2 1

ISBN 0 431 09111 0 (HB)
ISBN 0 431 09118 8 (PB)

British Library Cataloguing in Publication Data

Brunning, Bob
Jazz. - (Soundtrackers)
1. Jazz - Juvenile literature
2. Jazz musicians - Juvenile literature
I. Title
781.6'5

Printed and bound in Italy

Jazz

Bob Brunning

Heinemann
LIBRARY

CONTENTS

On these discs is a selection of the artist's recordings. Many of these albums are now available on CD. If they are not, many of the tracks from them can be found on compilation CDs.

These boxes give you extra information about the artists and their times. Some contain anecdotes about the artists themselves or about the people who helped their careers or, occasionally, about those who exploited them. Others provide historical facts about the music, lifestyle, fans, fads and fashions of the day.

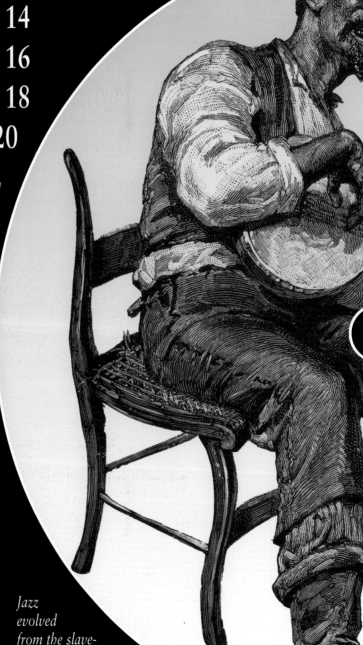

Jazz evolved from the slave-rhythms of the southern United States.

INTRODUCTION

Imagine if somebody asked you to explain exactly what rock music is. It would probably take you several hours to describe all the different styles and trends of the last 50 years. But jazz is even more varied – its history stretches back for a century. Jazz can mean anything from a solo bar-room pianist to the highly-orchestrated big bands of the 1930s, the 'cool' ensembles of the '50s and '60s or the raging electric bands of today.

Scott Joplin played an early version of jazz in the first years of the 20th century, ragtime – music played in a 'ragged' time or rhythm.

Jazz was the first all-American artform. It was entirely invented by black Americans, with no outside influences, except perhaps for the rhythms that slaves had introduced from Africa in previous centuries. No one doubts that there have been many distinguished white and non-American jazz musicians, some of whom are featured in this book. But unlike the blues, which was adapted and stylized by white performers in the 1960s, jazz remains the authentic music of black America.

It is impossible to make any serious study of jazz without understanding how most black Americans lived 100 years ago. They were subjected to bitter racism, segregation and poverty. Through music, they could attain dignity, a voice of their own and have a lot of fun at the same time! And because jazz proved popular with affluent white audiences, canny musicians could also earn a good living. The future of music was there for the taking.

LOUIS ARMSTRONG

It could be argued that Louis Armstrong was the most important figure in 20th century music. Single-handedly, he introduced improvization to jazz and invented many of the musical phrases which are taken for granted today. But Louis was not just a jazz musician. He was an all-round entertainer and singer, who enchanted millions, the world over. And he achieved all this from a background of almost unimaginable poverty.

BORN ON THE FOURTH OF JULY

'Hot Fives And Hot Sevens' 1925
'Satchmo At Symphony Hall' 1947
'Louis Armstrong Plays W.C. Handy' 1954
'Satch Plays Fats' 1955

'The Great Chicago Concert' 1956
'Ella And Louis' 1957, with Ella Fitzgerald
'Ella And Louis Again' 1957, with Ella Fitzgerald
'Ultimate Collection' 2000

Louis claimed that he was born on Independence Day 1900, a date that was patriotic, easy to remember and (conveniently) might have excused him from military service. Abandoned by his father, he grew up in the infamous ghetto of Storyville in New Orleans. He was sent away to reform school in his early teens for firing a handgun during a New Year's Eve celebration, and this punishment changed his life – the music teacher in the 'Colored Waifs Home' taught him to play the bugle and cornet. Louis was hooked. Free again, he started earning money as a musician, borrowing instruments and playing with any band that would have him. In about 1917, he joined the hottest and most successful band in New Orleans, led by cornetist King Oliver.

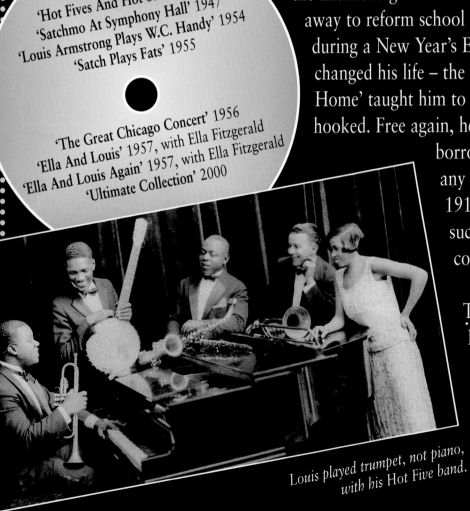

Louis played trumpet, not piano, with his Hot Five band.

THINGS HOT UP

He moved to Chicago with Oliver, and married the pianist in the band, Lillian Hardin. She encouraged him to head for New York. Over the next few years, Louis switched to trumpet and made classic recordings with his Hot Five and Hot Seven bands.

There are few trumpeters who have not been influenced by Louis's unique style.

HIGH SOCIETY

Louis Armstrong wasn't just a trumpeter and singer – he was an actor, too. His best-known screen appearance was in the 1956 movie 'High Society', which also starred Bing Crosby, Grace Kelly and Frank Sinatra. Louis memorably sang 'Now You Has Jazz'. Other songs included 'Well, Did You Evah' and 'Who Wants To Be A Millionaire?'.

Louis on the set of 'High Society' with stars Grace Kelly and Bing Crosby (far right).

ALL STARS

Nicknamed 'Satchmo', Louis fronted larger and larger bands over the next few years to great acclaim, and introduced his unique, gravelly singing to his act. By the 1940s, he was leading his All Stars, an ever-changing line-up of musicians, which included over the years Jack Teagarden, Earl Hines, Velma Middleton and countless others. Louis would continue to lead a succession of All Stars for the rest of his life.

Louis's funeral brought the streets to a standstill.

SATCHMO SELLS OUT?

As well as touring triumphantly, Louis made several film appearances, and had a number of hits in the pop charts, with songs such as 'Mack The Knife', 'Hello Dolly' and 'Cabaret'. Some jazz purists accused Louis of 'selling out', because of his popular appeal to white audiences, but the fact remains that he was a consumate performer. In 1968, he had a UK No. 1 hit with 'What A Wonderful World'. Against doctors' orders, Louis continued singing and playing into his seventies. He died in his sleep on 6 July 1971.

ORNETTE COLEMAN

In the 1920s, Louis Armstrong changed the face of music by inventing phrasing and styles that were imitated and adopted by everyone in jazz. Many artists have pushed jazz forwards, but there is probably only one other musician who can claim to have changed jazz single-handedly – Ornette Coleman. By carefully studying the music, Ornette tore up the rulebook that had governed jazz for 30 years, much to the horror of traditionalists!

JAZZ REBEL

In 1944, aged 14, Ornette Coleman acquired his first alto saxophone. At first, he thought that the low C on the instrument was the A in his instruction book, and although he realized his mistake in time, it made him examine new ideas in harmony and pitch. By 1946, he was playing tenor sax in various blues and R&B bands, and even with a touring minstrel show. So unusual was his style, that Ornette gained a bad reputation, and in 1949 he found himself stranded and jobless in New Orleans. Eventually Pee Wee Crayton took him into his band. When Ornette stubbornly refused to play traditonal blues, Crayton took him aside and told him in no uncertain terms that that was what he was being paid for!

Ornette Coleman switched back to alto saxophone, from the larger tenor instrument.

Ornette played trumpet on Jackie MacLean's 'Old And New Gospel'.

THE
ARRIVAL OF FREEFORM

Ornette took a number of day jobs, studying musical theory whenever he could. In the mid-1950s, he made contact with a number of musicians who sympathized with his ideas, and he established a quartet. A meeting with John Lewis of the Modern Jazz Quartet led to a two-week engagement at New York's Five Spot Café. Two weeks turned into a legendary 54-month stay, during which Ornette developed 'freeform', jerking jazz out of its 30-year love affair with chords. The Five Spot engagement saw him regularly vilified by the press and musicians alike, and even physically assaulted by an angry drummer. But enough people understood Ornette Coleman to turn him into a jazz hero.

STILL SHOCKING

In the 1960s, Ornette wrote some memorable film scores, notably 'Chappaque Suite'. The influence of rock began to creep into his work in the mid-1970s, as Ornette introduced electric guitars and basses into his band, Prime Time, which exists to this day. Even in the 21st century, many people consider freeform jazz to be outrageous and difficult on the ear. Others recognize Ornette Coleman's unique role in changing musical history, like it or not.

'Something Else!' 1958
'The Shape Of Jazz To Come' 1959
'Free Jazz' 1961
'At The Golden Circle, Volumes 1 & 2' 1966

'Science Fiction' 1972
'Of Human Feelings' 1982
'Beauty Is A Rare Thing:
The Complete Atlantic Recordings' 1993

JOHN COLTRANE

John Coltranc was one of the most gifted jazz musicians of all time. He was also an extremely intelligent and meticulous student of music, religion, philosophy, physics, mathematics and chess. Between his studies, he was a huge force for change in jazz, recording some seminal albums, and fronting the most acclaimed quartet in post-war jazz. He was already achieving legendary status, when his career was cut short at the age of 40.

EARLY PROMISE

John Coltrane was born in 1926, and brought up by his grandfather, the Reverend William Blair – John's religious faith remained very important to him throughout his life. He started out on clarinet, but rapidly switched to alto sax. After finishing high school, John won scholarships for performance and composition at a music school in Philadelphia, but it was in a navy band in 1945–6 that he honed his craft.

Out of uniform, John had spells in various big bands, notably Dizzy Gillespie's, and it was here that he adopted the larger tenor saxophone. A job in Miles Davis's classic 1955 quintet really got him noticed.

'Giant Steps' 1959
'My Favorite Things' 1961
'John Coltrane And Johnny Hartman' 1963
'Impressions' 1963
'Crescent' 1964
'A Love Supreme' 1965

'Ascension' 1965
'Transition' 1965
'Meditations' 1966
'Expression' 1967
'The Impulse! Years' 1993

John Coltrane played the straighter, high-pitched soprano sax on 'My Favorite Things'.

DOWN, BUT NOT OUT

John's tenor perfectly complemented Miles's trumpet, but Miles was forced to fire his sideman in 1957 because of his drug addiction. However, with admirable strength and personal courage, John managed to kick drugs and alcohol permanently, in just two weeks. The change was remarkable, and 'Trane' was able to develop his fluid, but rasping, style. He was back with Miles in 1959 for the classic album 'Kind Of Blue'.

THE PINNACLE

In 1960, John formed his famous quartet, with Jimmy Garrison on bass, Elvin Jones on drums and McCoy Tyner on piano. They recorded 'My Favorite Things', 'Impressions' and his finest album 'A Love Supreme', a musical celebration of the faith which had enabled him to overcome his addictions.

THE FINAL YEARS

After 'A Love Supreme', John embellished his band with more saxophonists, trumpeters and percussionists. To many, his music became increasingly inaccessible – Elvin Jones and McCoy Tyner both quit the fold. But John was keen to push back the frontiers of jazz. He was still doing this just weeks before his death in 1967.

AFRICAN BEAT

John Coltrane strongly believed that the origins of jazz were in Africa, and that black slaves had brought its percussive rhythms and harmonies with them to America in previous centuries. John helped to found the Olatunji Center of African Culture in New York City, and played at its opening in 1967 (below), complete with an ensemble featuring an African drummer. John was planning to make his first trip to Africa, to research its music and culture, shortly before his death.

John Coltrane embraced African sounds, such as the bata drum, pictured above.

John collaborated with Thelonious Monk and Duke Ellington over the years.

Freeform saxophonist Archie Shepp (left) was a regular with 'Trane' in the mid-1960s.

MILES DAVIS

When Dr Miles Davis gave his son a trumpet for his 13th birthday, could he have imagined that the boy would go on to be a master of the instrument and a jazz superstar? For over 40 years, Miles Davis Jr proved himself to be one of the most versatile and imaginative musicians ever, and perhaps the greatest bandleader in jazz. And he was responsible for an album which is still hailed as the greatest jazz record ever – 'Kind Of Blue'.

'Birth Of The Cool' 1957, recorded 1949–50
'Miles Ahead' 1957
'Milestones' 1958
'Porgy And Bess' 1959

'Kind Of Blue' 1959
'Sketches Of Spain' 1960
'In A Silent Way' 1969
'Bitches Brew' 1970
'Tutu' 1986

A PRICELESS EDUCATION

Born in 1926, Miles did not suffer a life of poverty or deprivation like so many of his peers. His dentist father was easily able to support his son through the prestigious Juilliard School of Music when he was 18, but the lure of New York's exciting jazz scene proved too strong, and he soon joined up with the legendary Charlie Parker. By 1948, Miles had worked with some of the greatest names in jazz – Coleman Hawkins, Benny Carter, Dizzy Gillespie, Gerry Mulligan and John Lewis.

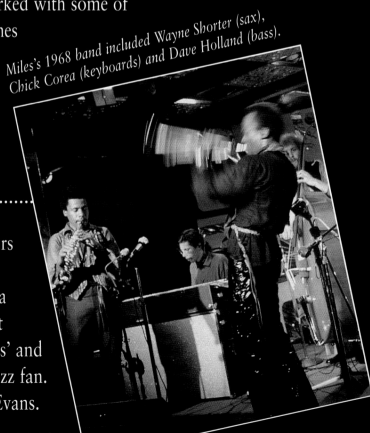

Miles's 1968 band included Wayne Shorter (sax), Chick Corea (keyboards) and Dave Holland (bass).

MILES AHEAD

Unfortunately, in the early 1950s, Miles became addicted to heroin, and his career stalled for a few years – there would be other lengthy periods of inactivity throughout his career. Back again in 1955, he formed a series of quintets and sextets, which included, amongst others, John Coltrane and Charles Mingus. 'Milestones' and 'Kind Of Blue' are essential listening for any serious jazz fan. He also recorded 'Porgy And Bess' with arranger Gil Evans.

During the 1980s, Miles was a regular at jazz festivals, such as that at Montreux, Switzerland (above).

ELECTRONIC JAZZ

Miles Davis was one of the great pioneers of electronic jazz. As early as 1968, he had electrified his band, and was playing his trumpet through an effect called a wah-wah pedal, just like rock guitarists Eric Clapton and Jimi Hendrix. Miles was dismissive of many rock musicians, but he influenced rock almost as much as jazz. On his disco-inspired album 'Tutu', he played his trumpet through a synthesizer.

Miles Davis also played electronic keyboards.

COOL JAZZ

Miles's restrained and economical style was given the label 'cool', to distinguish it from the pacy and furious playing of other artists. In 1965, Miles formed another fine band, which recorded 'E.S.P.', 'Miles Smiles' and 'Nefertiti'.

BUILDING ON A LEGEND

Miles continued to experiment through the early 1970s, constantly changing band-members and embracing new sounds. After a six year lay-off, he returned in 1981 with 'The Man With The Horn', and tackled pop and disco songs on his later albums. Miles spent the rest of his life recording and touring only when he felt like it, knowing his legendary status was assured. Despite his well-known health problems, the jazz world was shaken when Miles died in a Californian hospital in 1991.

DUKE ELLINGTON

Edward Kennedy Ellington was a pianist, composer, lyricist, bandleader and icon of the 20th century. Leading a succession of big bands for over 50 years, he brought sophistication and intricacy to jazz, which had mostly been thought of as rather shallow, lightweight music. Today, critics often compare the Duke with the greatest classical composers of the day.

CHILD PRODIGY

The Duke was born in 1899, and had a relatively comfortable upbringing – his father was a butler, and had served at the White House. His mother played the piano, and she encouraged him in his musical studies. By his mid-teens, he was writing tunes and playing for a living. By the age of 18, sharp-dressed and handsome, Duke Ellington was leading his first bands!

The Duke often used to shout "everybody look handsome" at his band!

The Duke owed much to his arranger Billy Strayhorn.

THE COTTON CLUB
Duke Ellington moved to New York in 1923, and soon formed the Washingtonians, who made a name for themselves in several nightclubs. In 1927, his band secured a residency at the Cotton Club in Harlem, which led to regular radio and recording sessions. Duke wrote some immortal tunes over the next few years, including 'In A Sentimental Mood', 'Satin Doll', 'Take The 'A' Train' and 'Don't Get Around Much Anymore', which influenced generations of musicians.

THE NEWPORT JAZZ FESTIVAL
Big bands seemed very old-fashioned by 1956, and Duke Ellington was struggling to keep his band going by the time of the Newport Jazz Festival that year. His musicians were in a stubborn mood when they took the stage at about midnight. Angry with them, Duke announced 'Diminuendo And Crescendo In Blue', a tune they hardly ever played. Something magical happened. Tenor sax-player Paul Gonsalves played no fewer than 27 solos, the crowd went wild, and until his death in 1974, the Duke was showered with awards, and hailed as a genius, all over the world.

Newport '56 didn't just change Duke Ellington's life – it changed the course of jazz.

THE FALL AND RISE OF THE BIG BANDS
The popularity of the big bands waned during the 1950s, but the Duke managed to keep his band on the road using his songwriting royalties. A triumphant performance at the 1956 Newport Jazz Festival brought him renewed success, and he was able to spend the rest of his life working on increasingly sophisticated orchestral suites with his loyal arranger Billy Strayhorn.

'The Indispensable Duke Ellington Vols 1–6', recorded 1927–40
'Ellington Plays Ellington' 1953
'Ellington At Newport' 1956
'Three Suites' 1960
'Duke Ellington Meets Coleman Hawkins' 1963
'Far East Suite' 1966
'70th Birthday Concert' 1969
'The New Orleans Suite' 1970

Duke Ellington was the ultimate showman, even in his seventies.

ELLA FITZGERALD

Dubbed 'America's First Lady of Song', Ella Fitzgerald gave the definitive performances of the work of America's foremost songwriters. Countless singers have tackled these songs, many of them successfully, but what singled Ella out was the young, fresh quality of her voice. And Ella was a jazz singer, first and foremost, as proven by her work with Louis Armstrong, Duke Ellington and Count Basie.

'Live From The Roseland Ballroom' 1940
'The Ella Fitzgerald Set' 1949
'The Cole Porter Songbook' 1956
'The Rodgers And Hart Songbook' 1956
'Porgy And Bess' 1956, with Louis Armstrong

'The Irving Berlin Songbook' 1958
'The George And Ira Gershwin Songbook' 1958
'The Harold Arlen Songbook' 1961
'The Jerome Kern Songbook' 1963
'The Johnny Mercer Songbook' 1964

BASHFUL BEGINNINGS

Ella was born in 1917, and moved to New York as a child. She showed early promise as a dancer, but her natural shyness was a hindrance. Nevertheless, Ella decided to enter a talent show. Frozen by stage fright, instead of dancing, Ella opened her mouth and sang. Her unexpected success led her to other contests, notably at the Harlem Opera House. Ella came to the attention of some major bandleaders, including Chick Webb, who took her on.

Amongst non-jazz audiences, Ella was the best-known and most popular jazz singer.

ELLA SPREADS HER WINGS

Ella became the star attraction in Webb's band, and after his death in 1939, took over as leader. She felt confident enough to start a solo career in 1942, and made some classic recordings. Along with Louis Armstrong, Ella developed 'scat' singing, an improvized vocal technique, using a stream of syllables, not words, to imitate musical instruments.

THE VERVE YEARS

In the late 1950s, Ella recorded a series of 'Songbook' albums for the Verve label, interpretations of classic American songs, or 'standards', which will probably never be bettered. She also recorded three joyous (and often hilarious) albums with Louis Armstrong, although the straight-laced Ella did not always appreciate Louis's larking in the studio!

AUTUMN YEARS

Ella continued to perform in concert halls and at festivals all over the world. It was only in the mid-1980s that her career finally came to a halt.

Ella had many collaborators, including Dizzy Gillespie.

Ella died at home in Beverly Hills in 1996.

NORMAN GRANZ

Norman Granz was one of the most powerful figures in jazz, yet he wasn't a musician. As a manager and producer, he always fought hard for the music he loved and for the rights of his artists. A fierce opponent of racism, he was instrumental in opening up concert venues, which had previously been closed to black artists. Granz was Ella Fitgerald's manager, and started the Verve label largely to promote her work. Other Verve artists included Oscar Peterson, Stan Getz, Dizzy Gillespie and Ben Webster.

Norman Granz started the successful 'Jazz at the Philharmonic' series of concerts.

DIZZY GILLESPIE

Along with Charlie Parker (see page 26), Dizzy Gillespie was a pioneer of a new kind of jazz in the mid-1940s, which was to influence the music for decades to follow. 'Bebop', or just plain 'bop', was truly revolutionary stuff. Characterized by fast and furious improvization, bebop owed little to traditional blues and jazz phrasing. It both enraged and thrilled audiences.

THE ORIGINS OF BEBOP

John Birks Gillespie began playing the trumpet in his early teens. Despite being mostly self-taught, he won a scholarship to study music, but preferred the life of a jazzman, and quit university in 1935. He was nicknamed Dizzy by a fellow trumpeter, because of his bubbly character. Dizzy's dazzling technique brought him plenty of work, and in 1937 he joined Teddy Hill's big band for a European tour. Back home in 1939, he joined up with drummer Kenny Clarke, who was also becoming disenchanted with the traditional big bands. Dizzy began to experiment with new jazz sounds, and in 1940, he recorded 'Hot Mallets' with Lionel Hampton's band – perhaps the first example of what would later be known as bebop.

Dizzy conducts his mid-1940s big band, which was not a great success.

NEW JAZZ, NEW TRUMPET

In 1940, Dizzy first met Charlie Parker, and they became friends over the next few years. Dizzy played with a huge variety of musicians, including Parker, until the early 1950s, constantly developing the bebop sound. Fate lent a hand in 1953, when his trumpet was accidentally damaged during a party, and the bell was bent at an upwards angle.

Amazingly, Dizzy found that when he played it, he preferred it that way, because his ear could pick up the notes more quickly. The bent trumpet became Dizzy's trademark.

JAZZ AMBASSADOR

Dizzy was highly respected, and not just in jazz circles. In 1956, US President Eisenhower sent Dizzy and his band on goodwill tours of Africa and South America. For the next 35 years, Dizzy led dozens of bands, big and small, around the world, and cemented his reputation as one of jazz's finest composers – 'Salt Peanuts', 'Hot House' and ' A Night In Tunisia' are all Gillespie originals. Dizzy died in 1993, aged 75.

Dizzy was loved for his jovial character, as well as for his music.

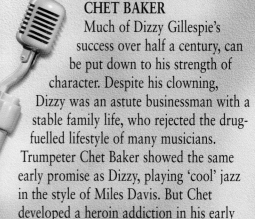

CHET BAKER

Much of Dizzy Gillespie's success over half a century, can be put down to his strength of character. Despite his clowning, Dizzy was an astute businessman with a stable family life, who rejected the drug-fuelled lifestyle of many musicians. Trumpeter Chet Baker showed the same early promise as Dizzy, playing 'cool' jazz in the style of Miles Davis. But Chet developed a heroin addiction in his early twenties, which would haunt him for the rest of his life. He died in 1988, aged 58.

Chet Baker fell to his death from an Amsterdam hotel window.

'Live At The Downbeat Club' 1947
'School Days' 1951
'At Newport' 1958
'Electrifying Evening' 1961
'Swing Low Sweet Cadillac' 1967

'Oscar Peterson And Dizzy Gillespie' 1974
'Trumpet Kings At Montreux' 1974
'Summertime' 1980
'To A Finland Station' 1982
'To Bird With Love' 1992

WYNTON MARSALIS

Every now and then, a group of musicians comes along to sweep away the movements of the last few years. Jazz in the 1970s was dominated by electric ensembles, playing a 'fusion' of rock and jazz. Even Miles Davis sometimes sounded as if he was playing pop music. Many fans thought it was time for jazz to get back in touch with its roots. Wynton Marsalis was the young trumpeter who spearheaded that change.

'Straight Ahead' 1981, with Art Blakey
'Think Of One' 1982
'Black Codes (From The Underground)' 1985
'J. Mood' 1985

'Standard Time' 1986
'Blue Interlude' 1992
'The All American Hero' 2000
'The Marciac Suite' 2000

Wynton has recorded the classical works of Haydn and Mozart.

OFF TO A GOOD START

Wynton, and his saxophonist brother Branford, came from an exceptionally talented family. Born in New Orleans in 1961, Wynton took up the trumpet aged six, encouraged by his father Ellis, a pianist, composer and teacher. Wynton studied classical music, but also developed an interest in jazz. In his teens, he was playing both with a marching band, and the New Orleans Philharmonic Orchestra. By the age of 19, he was a virtuoso, as well as a keen student of musical theory, jazz history and culture.

JAZZ PURIST

Wynton and Branford spent much of the early 1980s with Art Blakey's Jazz Messengers, and gained invaluable experience on the road. Wynton also played with jazz veterans Herbie Hancock and Ron Carter, and felt confident enough to form his own band, with Branford on tenor and soprano sax, and Kenny Kirkland on piano, both of whom would go on to play with the rock star Sting. But unlike Branford, Wynton was dismissive of rock music and jazz-rock fusion, and he strictly adhered to the 'hard bop' traditions of the 1950s and '60s.

DOUBLE AWARD-WINNER

Wynton continued to play classical music, and in 1984 became the first person to win Grammy awards for jazz and classical recordings in the same year. Wynton continues the fight to preserve jazz's heritage, while Branford presses ahead with experiments in jazz, hip-hop, blues and rock music.

ART BLAKEY AND THE JAZZ MESSENGERS

The Jazz Messengers, led by drummer Art Blakey, served as a university for young jazz musicians for over 30 years. Art had an uncanny knack of hiring young musicians, who would stay with him for a couple of years, then go on to stardom. Apart from the Marsalis brothers, ex-Messengers include Freddie Hubbard, Wayne Shorter, Herbie Hancock and Woody Shaw.

Art Blakey also guested with Thelonious Monk, Miles Davis and Charlie Parker.

Branford (left, with Wynton) was very influenced by John Coltrane.

Ellis Marsalis (above left) has become well-known through his sons.

CHARLES MINGUS

Jazz is full of contradictions. In the mid-1950s, bands were getting smaller – it was unusual to hear an act with more than six players. It seemed certain that the big bands of the '30s and '40s were on their last legs. Then along came an extraordinary bass-player, composer and arranger, who expressed himself not through a trio or quartet, but a big band – with a difference.

ANGER AND ALIENATION

Charles Mingus was born in 1922 into a mixed-race family – his grandparents were British-born, Chinese, Swedish and African American. This ancestry gave him feelings of persecution and paranoia, which would stay with him all his life. Influenced by European classical music and the sounds he heard in church, Charles went to study bass in New York.

BIG BANDS

The heyday of the big bands was in the 1930s and '40s. But although they went out of fashion, many of the big bands survived – even after the deaths of their leaders! Charles Mingus's big band continued under the name Mingus Dynasty, long after he had died. Count Basie's band carried on for a long time after his death in 1984. The bands of Glenn Miller and Duke Ellington each continued under the leadership of a relative. Glenn Miller's brother took over the famous wartime band for the next 50 years and the Duke was succeeded by his son.

Count Basie with Duke Ellington (right), whose son, Mercer, led the band after the Duke's death.

JAZZ WORKSHOP

Charles secured some dates with Kid Ory, Louis Armstrong and Red Norvo, and stunned audiences with his virtuosity. After a brief stint with Duke Ellington, he started his own record label, Debut, in 1953, to give black artists the exposure they deserved. 1955 saw the first of his experimental big bands, under the banner 'Jazz Workshop'.

Charles Mingus played at the Montreux Jazz Festival in 1975 with Gerry Mulligan on baritone sax (far right).

NOT SO SWEET SUCCESS

Charles Mingus's big band music differed from that of, say, Duke Ellington. It interspersed intricate, almost classical, passages, with manic improvization from the whole band. He mixed all manner of jazz styles, from New Orleans sounds to gospel, bebop and freeform. His amazing recordings brought him accolades and fame, but Charles remained bitter. He recalled how, after a show at New York's Carnegie Hall, he was unable to get home, because white taxi drivers refused to take him in their cabs.

STRUGGLING TO THE END

From the mid-1960s, the financial problems of running a big band started to affect Charles's mental health. 'Beneath the Underdog', his remarkable autobiography, revealed his inner turmoil when it was published in 1971. He continued to tour, until an incurable wasting illness prevented him from playing. In 1978, US President Carter honoured Charles with an all-star concert at the White House. The event moved him to tears. Early the following year, Charles Mingus was dead.

'Mingus Plays Piano', from 1963, is one of Charles's most interesting albums.

'Jazz Composers Workshop' 1954
'Pithecanthropus Erectus' 1956
'The Clown' 1957
'Mingus Ah Um' 1959
'Pre-Bird (Mingus Revisited)' 1960

'Oh Yeah' 1961
'The Black Saint And The Sinner Lady' 1963
'Mingus In Europe' 1964
'Let My Children Hear Music' 1971
'Cumbia And Jazz Fusion' 1976

THELONIOUS MONK

Teachers of classical music are always telling their students that they must learn certain rules and stick by them. Perhaps it was because Thelonious Monk only received formal piano tuition when he had already been playing for five years, that he never took the rules too seriously, playing with flat fingers, often hitting next-door keys at the same time. But if Thelonious had done as his teachers told him, he might never have become a genius of modern music.

DIVINE INSPIRATION

It was in 1924 that the six-year-old Thelonious Sphere Monk took up the piano. He was a bright student, excelling in maths and physics, as well as playing the organ in church. It was while touring with a gospel group that jazz beckoned, and he established a name for himself in the clubs, playing in Dizzy Gillespie's big band and with Coleman Hawkins.

Thelonious Monk led a string of quartets in the 1960s.

THE BLUE NOTE YEARS

In 1947, Thelonious entered the studios of Blue Note Records and recorded some inspirational sessions, with, amongst others, Art Blakey on drums. These recordings were eventually released on album and CD as 'Genius Of Modern Music', and it's easy to see why. They contain the first versions of Monk compositions, which went on to be jazz standards – 'In Walked Bud' and 'Ruby My Dear', for example. ''Round Midnight' is possibly the most widely-recorded song in jazz. Thelonious's unconventional piano style puzzled many listeners, but he was just trying to force sounds out of the instrument, which were usually only heard in eastern music.

Saxophonist Gerry Mulligan helped to promote Monk's music.

OUT OF THE PICTURE

In 1951, Thelonious was charged (probably falsely) with drug possession, and was banned for six years from playing in New York. This undoubtedly harmed his career, although he did find work outside the city. Back in 1957, he found the New York public more sympathetic to his music, and his career really took off in the 1960s. But ill health and natural shyness restricted his playing in the '70s. When Thelonious died in 1982, he had not played in public for six years.

'Genius Of Modern Music Vols 1 & 2'
recorded 1947–52
'Monk's Music' 1957
'Monk's Dream' 1962
'Big Band And Quartet In Concert' 1963

'Solo Monk' 1964
'Live At The Jazz Workshop' 1964
'Straight No Chaser' 1966
'Underground' 1967
'Blue Monk' released 1996

BUD POWELL
Bud Powell was another of bebop's supreme pianists. He was influenced by Monk's unusual style, but quickly developed a sound of his own. Bud played with all the major figures in bebop, including Charlie Parker and Dizzy Gillespie. But as a youth, he suffered a savage beating at the hands of the police, and this, coupled with addiction to drugs and alcohol, triggered a number of mental breakdowns. Bud was just 41 when he died in 1966.

Like Monk, Bud Powell recorded for the Blue Note label.

CHARLIE PARKER

Bebop's tragic hero, Charlie 'Bird' Parker set the jazz world alight when he emerged in the mid-1940s. Fellow musicians recalled the magical experience of hearing his alto saxophone for the first time. No one had imagined that one man could produce such amazing sounds. Bird has influenced every saxophonist who has come since. But his career hardly got off to a good start.

'Yardbird Suite' 1945
'Live At Rockland Palace' 1952
'Charlie Parker At Storyville' 1953
'Bird At The Hi-Hat' 1953

'Complete Dial Masters' released 2000
'Complete Savoy Masters' released 2000

PARKER PERSEVERES

Born in Kansas City in 1920, Charles Christopher Parker was given an alto sax by his mother when he was eleven. He dropped out of school at 14 to concentrate on the instrument, but his early stage performances were dogged by nerves. He froze during a solo at the Hi-Hat Club, and the humiliation prompted him to give up music for three months. In 1937, he was ordered off stage by drummer Jo Jones, but this time he resolved to practise harder. His efforts paid off, and by 1942 he was with Earl Hines's big band, along with his soulmate Dizzy Gillespie.

Bird formed a band with Miles Davis in 1947.

BIRD TAKES FLIGHT

Now known as Bird, he moved to Harlem in 1944 and hooked up with a number of like-minded musicians, including Thelonious Monk and, of course, Dizzy. Bird was so unusual because of the complex chords and rhythms his saxophone followed, his unbelievably fast solos and his use of the higher end of the instrument. Nothing like it had been heard before. After a handful of records were released, bebop became a national trend, and a celebration of everything young and fashionable.

OFF THE RAILS

But Bird was now an alcoholic and heroin addict, and after setting a hotel room on fire in 1946, he was imprisoned in the psychiatric wing of Los Angeles County Jail. Free in 1947, he made some classic recordings, and toured abroad for the first time, in France and Scandinavia. Bird even had a brief flirtation with classical music, as heard on the 'With Strings' albums. But ulcers and liver disease were the legacy of his hard lifestyle. Bird gave his last performance at Birdland, the club named after him, just a week before his lonely death in March 1955.

'BIRD'

The 1988 movie 'Bird' is a good starting point for anyone wanting to learn about the life and music of Charlie Parker. The star of the film, Forest Whitaker, had to take saxophone lessons, so that he could mime accurately to the music. The film pulls no punches in depicting Bird's genius, his downward spiral into drug addiction and his squalid death. 'Bird' was directed by Clint Eastwood, the actor who has often starred as gritty Wild West heroes and gun-toting policemen.

Forest Whitaker won the Best Actor award at the Cannes Film Festival for his performance in 'Bird'.

Tommy Potter (bass) played with Bird in the mid-1940s, along with Max Roach (drums).

Bird was given his nickname because he loved fried chicken!

WEATHER REPORT

The rock 'n' roll explosion of the 1950s and '60s passed jazz by. Jazz had Coltrane and Davis – why would it need Elvis and the Beatles? But by the late 1960s, rock music was so huge that it could no longer be ignored. Maybe jazz could learn from rock after all.

BEST OF BOTH WORLDS

Weather Report was one of the groups which invented jazz-rock fusion. It was formed in 1970 by Austrian keyboard-player Joe Zawinul and saxophonist Wayne Shorter, who had both played on Miles Davis's electric album 'Bitches Brew'. Realizing the potential of a rock-based rhythm section, they recruited Airto Moreira on percussion and Miroslav Vitous on bass. Their first album was a big hit, as were the group's high-energy live performances. Two more percussionists joined the band for their next album.

Joe Zawinul needed plenty of keyboards to produce the sounds he wanted.

BLUE SKIES AHEAD

By the time of the 'Sweetnighter' album, Joe Zawinul began to impose more structure on the group, moving away from freeform sounds, and giving more emphasis to melody. But Weather Report's live shows continued to be freewheeling displays of virtuosity, with each musician trying to outdo the others. The group was a revolving door for new jazz talent, as members came and went, with founders Joe and Wayne still at the core.

EVER-CHANGING, JUST LIKE THE WEATHER

Weather Report entered its most successful phase in 1976, when the flamboyant electric bass-player Jaco Pastorius joined the band. Instead of just providing rhythm, Jaco's bass served as a third lead instrument, as Joe experimented with the sophisticated electronic technology of the day. Their album 'Heavy Weather' even provided a hit, 'Birdland', which has become a jazz standard. With the arrival of Peter Erskine on drums in 1978, the group even had a stable line-up for a while. After another change of personnel in 1982, Weather Report continued for three years, before Joe and Wayne parted company, to pursue solo success.

Jaco Pastorius died a violent death outside a Florida nightclub in 1987.

STING

The rock star Sting had a problem in 1984. His band the Police was the biggest in the world, and had just completed a record-breaking world tour. But the band was effectively finished. How could he follow that? Sting decided to wipe the slate clean and get back to his jazz roots – he had started his career as a jazz bassist in Newcastle. He assembled the finest collection of young American jazz musicians he could find, including Omar Hakim, drummer with Weather Report, and Branford Marsalis. The resulting album, 'The Dream Of The Blue Turtles', was a worldwide smash, and it opened people's ears to a new sound – modern rock music played by jazz musicians. Sting continued the theme with 'Nothing Like The Sun' in 1987.

Sting played electric guitar, not bass, on his first solo album.

'Weather Report' 1971
'I Sing The Body Electric' 1972
'Sweetnighter' 1973
'Tail Spinnin' ' 1975
'Black Market' 1976

'Heavy Weather' 1977
'Mr. Gone' 1978
'8:30' 1979
'Night Passage' 1980
'This Is This' 1985

GAZETTEER

One of the most exciting things about jazz is its sheer variety. One person might adore the big bands. Another might go for 1970s freeform. They can fight like cats and dogs about which is better, but they are both jazz fans. Music by all the following artists is on CD, waiting to be discovered.

Bix Beiderbecke was rejected by his parents when he took up jazz.

Fats Waller made over 150 records.

WHITE JAZZ

Born in 1903, cornetist Bix Beiderbecke played with Paul Whiteman's orchestra but only achieved true recognition after his early death from chronic alcoholism in 1931.

STAR OF THE SLIDE TROMBONE

Trombonist Kid Ory was the first black New Orleans musician to make a record, in 1922. He was a champion of traditional jazz until his retirement in 1966.

Kid Ory quit music in 1933, but returned in the 1940s.

Grappelli was playing into his eighties.

Milt Jackson (far right) played vibraphone in the Modern Jazz Quartet.

Dave Brubeck worked with baritone sax-player Gerry Mulligan.

TRUE ORIGINAL

'Ain't Misbehavin' ', 'Honeysuckle Rose' 'Your Feet's Too Big' – just three in the long list of classic compositions by Thomas 'Fats' Waller. His lighthearted songs brought some welcome relief during the dark days of unemployment and economic depression in the 1930s.

FOREIGN STARS

It's not just America that's produced some great jazz. Parisian violinist Stéphane Grappelli and Belgian guitarist Django Reinhardt formed the Quintette du Hot Club de France in the early '30s. Their style of jazz has been much imitated, but never bettered. Gil Evans was born in Toronto, Canada. As well as his arrangements for Miles Davis (see page 12), Gil made a number of records under his own name.

Stan Getz was one of the most highly-regarded tenor-players ever.

JAZZ SAMBA

Tenor sax star Stan Getz brought the Brazilian 'samba' style of music to jazz, through his work with Antonio Carlos Jobim. 'The Girl From Ipanema' became a worldwide hit for them.

Gil Evans also worked with Sting.

MODERN JAZZ

The expression 'modern jazz' was first coined in the 1950s – people have been struggling to think up a more up-to-date term ever since! Dave Brubeck irritated some jazz purists by putting a modern jazz tune into the top 10 in 1961, but 'Take Five' remains instantly recognizable all those years later. Milt Jackson, John Lewis, Percy Heath and Connie Kay, the Modern Jazz Quartet, performed their brand of (not so modern) music for 35 years. Today, jazz is still a modern and evolving artform. Who knows what's around the corner?

INDEX